Astrology

Locked

Down

Astrology

Locked Down

Through the Lens of Astrology,

We Take a Candid Look

at the

Events of 2020 and

Beyond

Charlotte Rudge

Author: Charlotte Rudge
Cover Design: iBUZZLink
Book Design: iBUZZLink
ISBN: 9798727228418

https://astrobabies.wordpress.com
astrobabies@gmail.com
www.instagram.com/astrologylockeddown

This book is not intended as a substitute for the medical advice of physicians or doctors. The reader should regularly consult a physician in matters relating to his/her health and particularly with respect to any symptoms that may require diagnosis or medical attention.

*I wish to dedicate this book to all of those
that have not made it through the past year,
and to those who have got us through it.*

Thank you to all of my friends and family.

*A special thank you to Adrian, for all of his
love and support with the writing of
Astrology Locked Down. I could not have
done it as well without you.*

*So much love to my two wonderful children,
Hollie and Jago, who have given me the
motivation and inspiration to write this book
in the first place.*

*And of course, I am eternally grateful to our
ever-powerful Universe for providing me
with the blessings I receive every day.*

Introduction

As a relationship and family astrologer, together with identifying as an avid self-proclaimed psychology geek, the unfolding events of the world in the previous twelve months have been fascinating to watch. To observe how different people have coped with these unprecedented times, and how the influence of the planetary transits has affected us all as a global community in such a deep and integral way, has been captivating. It is almost as if we have been thrust into a huge, world-wide social experiment, a 'Big Brother' type scenario with our nearest and dearest! As with everything experienced in life, I have been reflecting on how I have personally dealt with these lockdown situations, my own reaction to the virus and also, how this strange set of circumstances have impacted on my personal relationships. Then, as I tend to do, I began pondering these same questions through the lens of my natal astrology chart. After which, I turned my attention to those around me and began observing how everyone has coped and reacted to the changing times, the uncertainty, and the endless stream of upheaval sweeping the world.

Although I would not claim to be a skilled predictive astrologer, I have been keeping a close eye on all of the strong and life-altering transits of the past year and, in doing so, I have learnt a lot about the power and accuracy of the universe. What Astrology enthusiast does not want to know about the astrological influences that have impacted us in such a big way?!

The astrological transits of the past twelve months have been building up for at least three years previous to this. I have felt them impact my own life, and I have seen the big players in the skies impact everyone around me too.

As I set out to write this book about the zodiac signs and their individual reactions to the crazy events of 2020, I realised that it was not complete without a part two and three. I needed to write a second part, to attempt to make sense of the events of the pandemic during 2020, and a third section to share my personal predictions for the year ahead in 2021 for the world. And so, this book has effectively become a three in one. The first part is a light-hearted overview of how each of the zodiac signs are handling the pandemic and the lockdowns.

Part two is a look at the history of the Pluto-Saturn conjunction in Capricorn, and a deep dive into the astrological transits that have impacted the world and every one of us during this past year. Part three is a conclusive analysis of the coming year so that you will have a better understanding of what is in store for our global community.

Part 1

The Pandemic

and You

Each of the zodiac signs react differently to stress, change, and being thrust into an unparalleled new world of novel viruses, leading to heightened germ-phobia, anxiety, depression, extreme isolation, huge economic changes, working from home, home educating our children, as well as the ultimate relationship test of being with our loved ones around the clock!

Analysing my natal chart and focusing on my personal planets of Libra on the Ascendant, Sun and Mercury in Virgo, Moon in Cancer and Venus and Mars in Leo, I could see that my reaction was typical of what these signs would be like and that through examination of your personal planets through astrology, you could predict how it is directly impacting on how you and I, are responding to these seemingly endless series of lockdowns and the virus itself.

Being an astrologer, I naturally have tabs on everyone I know. Not only knowing birthdays, but their time and place of birth, which gives me access to their natal charts at the click of a button, and in turn, an insight into their inner workings.

If you want a better insight into your personal outcomes, then I highly recommend finding your own natal chart for free on astro.com before reading this book. It is simple to use and free. Just as an example of how this is useful, I have written a short description of my own natal chart in relation to these events below.

Early on, the new rules suited my Cancer Moon quite nicely! I liked that I could spend time with myself, without the social pressures of having to meet up with other people regularly. I was quite happy to be at home with my children, indulging in cooking some new (and old favourite) recipes, while away my days in the garden over the summer months, and snuggle up on the sofa watching Netflix in the darker, colder months. After the initial shock at being thrown into a world-wide pandemic, I enjoyed having the extra time at home, so I initially adjusted very quickly.

My Virgo side was fairly content too! I liked having the extra time to write more, and to do the things that I do often get pulled away from in the flow of everyday life before the pandemic. There seemed to be a huge boost in online courses and learning that I could engage my analytical mind with whenever I felt the urge. Through these lockdowns, I have also had a lot of time to work at home and write more of what I love, such as this astrology book! I have also enjoyed having the time to do lots of outstanding home improvements. My lists have become a perfect distraction and I have revelled in ticking off my endless to do's!

However, as many people do, I have a contrast to these aspects of myself, and having Libra Rising, and Mars and Venus in Leo, means that I am driven by social interactions, and do enjoy the company of other people. I began to miss engaging in novel conversations, having a reason to get dressed and making myself look nice every morning and going to the odd social event! As you can see from the above description, we are much more complex than just our Sun sign!

Every placement and aspect combine to create a complex and multifaceted person. To find your personal natal chart, please refer to astro.com and put in your details to generate the chart that will show you where the Sun, Moon, Ascendant and other planets were when you were born.

Analysing my own reaction through the lens of Astrology, as well as the transits that have contributed and led to this pandemic in the first place, has led me to write this book; to let you all know that you are certainly not alone in your reaction to being locked up and isolated from the people you love, no matter what your sign may be!

I have written this with the presumption that most of us are working and/or spending much of our time at home, unable to go out other than for our daily exercise, to the shops for essentials, and from the perspective of both; being at home alone, barely in physical contact with anyone, and that we may be spending lockdown with someone else. In this way, I thought it would also be interesting to include a section on what it might be like to be locked up with each sign, as well as what each sign is like if they have (a mild version) of the virus!

In these situations, there are many factors to consider, and everyone has had their own experience of this pandemic. Some of us have lost loved ones, and if that is you, I am truly sorry for your loss. This would clearly have an impact on us beyond what I am writing here, and I have not included that as a factor.

Most of us by now have had enough, considering we have basically lost a year, and we had pinned our hopes on 2021 being different, but frustratingly, it has carried on into the new year and into Spring, not set to change significantly until June in the UK!

So how have you handled the past year? Let us find out according to your Sun sign, and any other dominant signs you have within your personal natal chart...

Here goes the first part of the book, with the intention of a little light-hearted fun during the despair!

From Aries to Pisces how do you relate to the following descriptions?

Aries

Aries

ASTRO BABIES

Initially Aries, you were outraged at those in charge telling you what you can and cannot do! You probably reacted with fury and frustration. You may well have been one of the many that defied the lockdowns all together! However, after a few heated posts and perhaps a few debates on social media, or just a good rant to your significant other, you soon cooled off and decided to change tactics and use the lockdown as a way of starting a new venture, utilizing the time to challenge yourself in a new way. Maybe you started a new business, a hobby that you previously did not have time for, or a new workout regime? Whatever it was, during the first lockdown you attacked it with vigour and were super busy building your new venture! However, by Christmas you had had enough! I imagine you went ahead with your plans regardless of the rule changes. If you had plans that needed to be changed, then you made a new plan and went with that. No one stops you once you have decided what you want to do!

During this lockdown, you have had quite enough of being controlled and dictated to. I would say many of you are raring to go and may have broken lockdown regulations more than once. Aries is not the best at sticking to the rules, often they do not even remember them, because they tend to live by their own rules and feel that the rules simply do not apply to them! Masks? You often just forget to wear them, or just refuse because you do not like the feeling of them on your face.

Those of you who are still home, are thoroughly fed up now. You miss your fast pace of life, and just wish that everything would return to the status quo!

If you have been a key worker throughout the pandemic, you have adapted quickly and attacked your role head on with bravery. With rolled up sleeves and a deep breath, your 'let's get on with it' attitude is admiral, considering many have been worried about going out and catching the virus.

Aries under attack from the virus? – Total shut down!

When Aries get sick, they tend to get really sick! They tend to want around the clock care and attention... While you are usually fearless and up for anything, sickness takes everything out of you.

Even if it is just a case of the sniffles, you will want to spend every moment in bed and could not possibly get up to get yourself a drink or food, you need to be waited on hand and foot.

You are the first to admit you go into full baby mode when you are ill, but once you are better, you will be able to take on the world again.

Arrested with an Aries?

If you have spent the lockdown with an Aries, then I would say you are more than ready for it all to end right now! As much as you love them, they like things done their way, and I do not suppose you realised quite how bossy and demanding they were before spending every minute, of every day with them.

On the other hand, Aries being the self-motivated sign that they are, may well have used this time spent at home to start a new venture.

You could definitely feel inspired by your Aries lockdown buddy to get creative with your own ideas which is the perfect boost to your motivation too.

Aries being the independent type, needs their space and to have their own separate thing going on, other than their relationship with you. This can put a strain on you if you are a social, cuddly type of person that usually get that top up from other friends and family members. Bear in mind that nobody is their best selves right now.

Once they are able to get out and do their thing again, their energy will be directed elsewhere, and an equilibrium will be restored... Well as much as a relationship with an Aries can be on an equilibrium!

Missing most?

The freedom to do what you want. And the gym.

Enjoying most?

Having the time to start something new!

Initial reaction to the virus?

Not really bothered or it is probably not real!

Opinion on the lockdown?

Ridiculous, what about our freedom to make our own minds up?

Thoughts on the future?

I will be OK so long as I can get back to my life soon.

Taurus

Taurus

ASTRO BABIES

When the lockdown happened, you looked in the cupboard, fridge and freezer and assessed the stores. If you had the means to do so, you were the people that decided to stockpile... If you did not do it initially, you could well have been one of the many that went to the supermarket and stripped the shelves to hoard enough food and essentials for you and your family.

To a Taurus, food is life after all! If you have some good food to eat, and your home comforts around you, you are happy.

During the first lockdown, you probably put on a little bit of weight as you took the opportunity to eat comfort food and binge watch Netflix!

If you had to give up work, you probably worried mostly about money and how you were going to survive without your full income. However, you soon got yourself into a groove and started to look forward to your daily walks, cooking your favourite meals, and spending some time in the garden, or curled up reading a good book.

You may have started a little herb garden and by the end of the summer, if you did not have one before, you had quite the sustainable vegetable garden.

Because of your calming demeanour you have probably been a great support and good listening ear to those of your friends and family who may have struggled through the lockdowns.

During the second lockdown, you really did begin to wonder how you were going to earn some money and you hope to god that your favourite restaurant was not one of the ones that was set to close because of the economic stresses of the pandemic.

You wished that you had more time to prepare pre-Christmas, as you had made your plans for the festive season and feel that the government changes gear way to often for you to keep up with!

This changeable element has been most annoying to you! By now you may have started some kind of side hustle and be well on your way to launching it once this damn lockdown ends!

Have you been a key worker throughout the past year Taurus? If so, you will have struggled with all of the changes initially, but by now you are in the swing of things and feeling good about helping the nation to keep going. You are naturally caring, and you will have been a rock for your fellow co-workers when they were struggling. Home-made cakes are always a winner to cheer everyone up.

Taurus caught the virus? Takes care of themselves.

Taurus do not let a little thing like illness take them down for too long. You know that even if you have a lot to get done, the best thing to do is to get plenty of rest and fluids and take things easy until you get better.

You know people depend on you, but that you cannot help anyone else until you have helped yourselves. You tend to recover from being sick lickety-split.

Trapped with a Taurus?

If you were locked up with a Taurus dominant person, you probably found them quite easy to be around, so long as you did not try and change the routine and stop their over-indulgences.

They may have had the odd bull in a china shop moment and lost their temper a couple of times at the shear suddenness of the changes, but overall, other than a couple of little love handles, they are pretty much the same as they always were, for better or worse!

Missing most?

The security of a steady income and stable future.

Enjoying most?

Having the time to slow down and do the things you enjoy doing.

Reaction to the virus?

You were quite stressed by the sudden changes and the 'not knowing' what was happening and when.

Opinion on the lockdown?

It has turned out ok, and probably a necessity.

Thoughts on the future?

Perhaps slowing down and having more time to cook and go for nice walks is not such a bad thing.

Gemini

Gemini

ASTRO BABIES

Gemini, this is a kind of torture previously unknown and because you need a lot of intellectual stimulation and kinetic movement, you have especially found the lockdowns during winter a total drag.

I would say your mental health has suffered quite a lot throughout the second lockdown and even during the first one, a 30-minute walk was just never going to cut it for super active Gemini's!

Within the first lockdown, you probably checked everything of your to-do list within the first month, rearranged the furniture, watched everything that you had saved on Netflix, talked to every old friend and distant relative you could think of, and then felt as though you were going to go insane for the remainder of the lockdown!

If you did manage to stick to the first one, the second one proved that much harder as you knew what was coming.

As the fact-checker of the zodiac, you may well have put your cool-head on and decided that you were going to help the world by forwarding the news updates via social media, writing that blog you always wanted to start, or starting a podcast.

Keeping a journal and recording your quarantine experience for your own sanity, or even to share in a blog may be a big help to you. Plus, people love to relate and knowing they are not alone will be a service to humanity.

If you are a key worker throughout the lockdowns Gemini, you probably found it a relief you have still been allowed to get out, even if it has just been for work. You may have had your anxious moments about catching the virus and being knocked off your feet for a couple of weeks, but overall, you have enjoyed mucking in and keeping your mind occupied with your work.

Gemini got germs? – Feels like they will never be well again!

Poor Gemini. This friendly, sociable sign does not cope well with sickness. They tend to feel especially unwell when they get sick, and in addition to feeling poorly, they tend to feel like they are missing out and the world is moving on without them, when they must stay home.

They would much rather be spending time with friends and catching up with everything going on in the world, which makes them feel even sicker. But just when being sick starts to feel like the status quo, they get better.

Jailed with a Gemini?

If you spent your lockdown with a Gemini, god help you! No, I am joking of course... They may well have driven you mad with their changeable mood, multiple personalities, need for constant stimulation, or their quick descent into insanity, but you will also have been entertained by their wit and endless chatter.

In their brighter moments, they will have made up some fun games and you may well have got even closer to your Gemini friend as you will have finally been able to pin them down!

You may well have felt inspired by their energy, and drive to get things done, and to channel their busy mind into something amazing.

Missing most?

Being free to do what you want spontaneously. Seeing friends, going to the gym, bar, party, or taking an unplanned road trip to the beach.

Enjoying most?

Having the time to chat with friends and family, write that blog, or start that at home fitness routine.

Initial reaction to the virus?

You hate getting ill, so you were quite worried at first, but as time went on you just wanted to get back to your fun life, minus the virus!

Opinion on the lockdown?

It is probably causing more harm than good!
People have lives to live, people to see, and
places to go! Mental health is important too.

Thoughts on the future?

If this continues, there is no future! Maybe,
we need to all just calm down! Wait, no, I
need to calm down... I have not got a clue
what the future holds. (Holds head in hands).

Cancer

Cancer

ASTRO BABIES

You are most likely to be one of the signs in the zodiac that has actually enjoyed spending more time at home!

Cancer Sun, Moon or Rising have all quickly settled into a homely routine, and loved that any pressure to be sociable, and away from their home, has literally been squashed by the virus! I imagine this is what they wish the world is like all of the time - minus the virus of course!

You are quite prone to worry though Cancer, and this past year could have sent your anxiety levels through the roof as you worry about the economy, lack of stability for your immediate family, as well as your more vulnerable family members.

Other than this though, so long as you have your family around you, you have been quite happy to be under house arrest!

You have rediscovered your love for cooking, finding new and rediscovering old recipes, as well as having everyone in attendance for family meals. You have loved spending more time in bed clothes, without the usual social pressure to be dressed daily, you totally dived into the 'pj's everyday' trend.

You have enjoyed your time snuggling on the sofa, watching Netflix, and eating popcorn. You have probably driven your children mad with all of the cuddles and the 'extra happy' love you have had to give!

Just be aware that if you have a Cancer friend or relative that is spending lockdown's alone, then be sure to check in on them daily. You are definitely prone to develop depression if you do not have your dose of physical affection regularly.

Cancer got Covid? - Pile on the sympathy!

Cancer is an empathetic and emotional sign, and when they are sick, it really helps when they feel like others are warmly sympathetic to their plight.

They make their illness known, but for a good reason. They feed off of positive vibes, and when they feel like people really care for them, they will recover faster than most.

Confined with a Cancerian?

If you have spent your lockdowns with a Cancerian, you will probably recognise these traits during the first lockdown... however by now, although they are still happy to be at home, you will have experienced the mood swings like never before!

Although they have you, they will be missing their other close connections and the physical closeness that they need, can never be filled up by one person.

Another issue you may have found, is the constant need for reassurance about the virus itself. They will probably have developed anxiety about going out of their bubble and, for those that have had to, they will be very anxious at times about losing someone they love or dying themselves.

By now their emotions will have been up and down so often, that it is hard to know what they need from you at any given moment!

That being said, the love, support, and physical closeness will have grown between you through the lockdowns, and they will be a great comfort to you whenever you have had a wobble.

The problem has been for those Cancerian's that are living alone. If this is you, the lockdowns have probably been a form of torture!

Not being able to see your mum, or your own children has been excruciating. Zoom just does not cut it for you as you need the physical cuddles! You were certainly the ones over Christmas saying 'what's the point in living 'if we can't be with family at Christmas!?'

Missing most?

Physical contact, their mum's, or children if you are not living together.

Enjoying most?

The lack of social pressure to go out of your comfort zone.

Initial reaction to the virus?

You have a very real anxiety about catching it... Barricades themselves in their homes... 'woohoo, this is nice!'

Opinion on the lockdown?

It is a blessing in disguise and allows us all to reconnect and slow down... Or, omg I cannot see my mum or my kids?! No one can keep us apart!

Thoughts on the future?

It has shown us we should all reconnect with our family and stay home/work from home more. I do not want the world to go back to the way it was.

Leo

Leo

ASTRO BABIES

For you Leo, this moment in time is called 'the captive audience'. During the first lockdown, and with your ability to put a positive spin on everything, you have enjoyed the fact that everyone is home. All. The. Time! And because they are at a loss to fill the hours, the least you can do is keep their spirits high with some grade A entertainment!

Apart from an all-you-can-eat buffet of attention at home, you have been the entertainers for the world at large... Especially for those of you living solo through the pandemic, everyone else is at home too, and they are scrolling, endlessly! Instagram reels and TikTok were made for you Leo, and this is exactly your moment to shine, entertain and take people's minds off the pandemic.

For the creatives out there, the world is your oyster with live stream music, performing arts, and YouTube videos galore, it is time to bring what you have got to offer and put it out there!

However, as the sunshine dwindled and the dark nights began drawing in, you started to lose some of your sparkle and positivity. Depression may have been a big factor for you during the latter half of the past year and it is important to talk to your loved ones about how you are feeling.

Not having the ability to leave the house in your sparkly dress and have the feeling of all eyes on you as you walk into a party, club, bar, or even your workplace or school has been an absolute downer for you.

As we move into Spring again, you may begin to pick up, and regular zoom calls and socially distanced walks have got you through Leo. Keep going and try to find an outlet for your love and kindness in helping through this difficult time.

If you have been a key worker throughout this past year, you may well have kept your spirits a little higher, as you really do thrive in times of need. You have a big heart Leo, and you want to be of help to those in need. You like to be the one that cheers people up and gives people hope and inspiration. Just be your amazing self and you will inspire people around you to follow suit too.

Leo got the lurgy? Never admits they are sick!

People-pleasing, crowd-loving Leos just do not think they can afford to get sick. Even when their noses are visibly running and they can barely keep their eyes open, they pretend nothing is wrong and keep on moving.

They do not want to admit to themselves that they are susceptible to illness, and they definitely will not let it on to anyone else. This can wind up making them even sicker, but still then, they will not give in.

Locked up with a Leo?

At first, Leo was a breath of fresh air and kept you more than entertained and happy. Sure, they had the odd dramatic outburst, of 'OMG we're all going to die' moments, but mostly they focused on making themselves stand out on their social media platforms and brought a lot of joy and happiness.

During the Winter lockdown, they may well have sunk into a darker mood. Winter is not Leo's best season. They miss the sunshine and crave a lot of attention, affection, and to give of themselves to others, to be needed in a way that is near on impossible to be fulfilled by just one person!

Once the days get longer and the springtime kicks in, you will see your ray of sunshine come back to life and return to a happier version of themselves. Hang in there!

Missing most?

The parties, the fun times, the groups that you attended BC (before Covid!)

Enjoying most?

The drama of it all! Being the light bringer for people, having time to create for your most captive audience yet!

Initial reaction to the virus?

I am sure that it is going to be fine and will just pass over like many other viruses in the past... But obviously, I DO NOT want it!

Opinion on the lockdown?

It sucks! But my Instagram following is SOOO high now!

Thoughts on the future?

Needs to be better than this... We need to find new and interesting ways to help keep everyone in high spirits, whatever the future holds.

Virgo

Throughout the lockdowns, you have probably stayed the most balanced of all of the signs. You had your initial freak out, but after digging into some research and adjusting your supplements accordingly, you feel ready to take it on! It is as though you have been preparing for this your whole life through!

Stringent hygiene and being healthy is trending, and you usually have a couple of bottles of hand sanitiser in your handbag as a matter of course. In the early days, when the pandemic hit you made sure to buy your essentials well in advance, beforehand sanitizer and toilet roll became like gold dust.

The nation's new focus on bench spraying and hand washing will have you feeling like the world has finally caught on to what you already know. While you can be tightly wound due to your finely tuned nature, in many ways this is your time to shine. Built to see the potential improvement in any situation or person, you will know just what to do to help out, which in turn will take your mind away from a natural propensity to worry.

Need sanitizer, leave it up to you Virgo to know how to DIY with some alcohol and blended aloe pulp from your balcony garden.

As the lockdowns continue, you are trying to stay motivated and are making new lists to continue your self-improvement marathon! Setting up your stay-at-home routine to keep the day ticking along is the way forward. It is when your routine goes astray that you struggle.

The winter months have been a drag for all of us, and your daily exercise routine has had to move indoors whilst the rain and snow are visiting. This can be depressing as you enjoy getting out into nature, and there is only so much organising, cleaning, writing, reading, and studying one Virgo can do! Hang in there, Virgo... It will soon be over.

If you have been a key worker during these difficult times, you will have worried, a lot! However, you naturally want to help others and to be of service, so this will over-ride the worry and anxiety you might be feeling whilst in your role. You will do all you can to ensure that everyone that you are working with is kept safe through your high standards of hygiene and cleanliness. You may well be the go-to person for advice on how your colleagues can up their game with their personal health, general well-being, and strengthen their immune system.

Virgo got the Virus? - Keeps it to themselves!

When a Virgo gets sick, they do not think it is anybody's business but their own. They take extra vitamins and rest in their free time, but they tend to continue on with life like everything is normal. This careful balance does not always work out, but Virgo believes it is important to keep the ball rolling no matter what.

Because of Virgo's super healthy lifestyle, they tend to fight most viruses off with ease. They do not just grab the vitamins when times are tough, they have been taking them on schedule since they were young. They eat their vegetables and avoid junk food, and this stands them in good stead with this new virus as well. At the end of it, you would never have known that Virgo was sick in the first place.

On the Verge with a Virgo?

During the first lockdown, your Virgo housemate may have become a tad hypervigilant and stressed out by the thought of a new virus sweeping the world! They may have needed a lot of reassurance and initially, they are anxious for you to stick to the rules… Not just the government guidelines, but their extra cautious rules too.

Once they have had some time to process and do some research into the ins and outs of the virus and readjust their supplements after looking at what works and what does not, they will have relaxed a bit and turned their attention to how to make the most of being at home and not at work.

They will have a list of things they want to achieve, not just for themselves but for you too. You will have lots of chores to complete, they may have a strict routine that they adhere to, for work, school, and leisure activities. Your Virgo will inspire you to do the same and utilise the lockdowns to your maximum benefit.

Missing most?

If you are off work, then you miss your daily routines, otherwise you are pretty ok.

Enjoying most?

The time to take life a little slower, get on top of some chores and jobs that you wanted to do, creating whole new routines and rituals. You are quite comfortable.

Initial reaction to the virus?

Worry and stress. But then you realised you feel well equipped to handle it.

Opinion on the lockdown?

It is necessary, and we can all get through it if we just stick to the rules and do it properly!

Thoughts on the future?

People should learn from this and consider being more prepared. Get healthy, follow good hygiene, and learn to adapt.

Libra

During the first lockdown, you were suddenly thrust into a world that is almost the opposite of everything you need to thrive in life Libra! The only saving grace during the initial isolation was that we still had the weather to get out for our daily walks and to connect with all things beautiful in the natural world.

Another thing that will have helped you through is if you have had a loved one or best friend at home to keep you company, the lockdown will not have been so bad. You thrive in harmonious environments Libra, so you will have been totally unbalanced from the scare stories on the news and by other people's fear and stress surrounding the virus. Try to avoid listening to it all and you will fare much better.

Libran's do not do well without daily contact, so if you do not have someone to share the long, countless hours of winter's lockdown with, consider sitting this isolation out at a friend or family's place. The only caveat to this suggestion, is if the environment is not a harmonious one. Libran's need peace and tranquillity to feel happy and well-balanced, so you will struggle if you are stuck in with someone confrontational, too messy, or stressy!

Air signs need to talk, and Libra is the sign associated with counselling, so you will be kept more than busy talking your stressed-out friends back off the ledge and into a calm. This could be the perfect time to start your internet-based therapy business!

If you have been struggling mentally then remember that Libra is ruled by the planet of love and beauty, break out your paint set, or tune-up your instrument, this is the perfect time to indulge your artistic side.

If you have been on the front line during this past year Libra, you may well have felt your moods swinging from up to down and totally unbalanced by all of the turmoil that is going on in the world. You are quite sensitive to other people's stress. If your colleagues have been supportive and positive, then you will have followed suit, and if not, you may have struggled with being out there.

One of the positives of working through the lockdown's has been the social aspect. You have enjoyed the comradery and the daily contact with others, even if it has not always been good. You are also quite happy to be involved in anything that fights for social justice and fairness Libra, so if you feel that your work has been in alignment with that feeling, you will have felt proud of your role within that.

Feeling low Libra? Complains a lot but gets on with it!

Libra is perfectly capable of fulfilling every one of their duties, even when they are under the weather, but you would not necessarily know that based on how they talk about their sickness. They are social creatures, and when it comes to them being poorly, misery loves company.

Based on a Libra's complaints, you might think things are way worse than they actually are. However, venting is just their way of feeling better and making it through the day.

They will soon be as right as rain if given enough sympathy and feel listened to.

Feeling limited with a Libra?

So, your locked up with your usually balanced and social butterfly Libra friend? This has been a tough job for you to keep their spirits up and you have had to play a supporting role throughout. Social contact with others for a Libra is not something they do for pleasure; it is a deep need in them and without it they wither and die!

Despite this, they have really come through in supporting others in their darkest hours and hidden their own torment pretty well from the world. It is only because you are with them every day that you see them swinging from one extreme to the other in their despair. This is a sad situation to watch, and I am sure you have tried to rally them up as much as you can do through suggesting online groups, telephone calls, and socially distanced walks in the park with friends.

The second lockdown has been especially tough for Libra and so all we can do is keep reminding them to do the things that bring them joy and balance. Help them to get in touch with their creativity and this can be a lifeline for their declining mental health.

Missing most?

Social interactions, meeting new people, being with friends and going to nice places.

Enjoying most?

Having time to get in touch with your artistic side.

Initial reaction to the virus?

First it was worry, but you soon composed yourself and became the rock and a listening ear for your friends who were struggling.

Opinion on the lockdown?

You swing from it is for the best and coping well, to not coping well at all!

Thoughts on the future?

We will adapt and overcome this, no matter the future, we need to get back to some form of social life.

Scorpio

Scorpio

ASTRO BABIES

Scorpio, you knew this day would one day come, and are probably not surprised in the slightest with how this pandemic has played out. Not that you were prepping like a Virgo or anything!

A mask and dark sunglasses suited your look and need for privacy in the beginning. Perhaps, in a weird way you felt quite excited by the mystery surrounding the beginnings of the virus, and you may have found watching the reactions of the people around you quite fascinating.

You may have spent the first part of the year enjoying some respite from daily contact with others. Being a water sign, you are sensitive to the energies of other people, and to atmospheres. For you, spending time alone for a while was not difficult.

Apart from that, staying in your ambiently lit boudoir, with a book on the latest metaphysical musing is historically your idea of a cosy night in during the winter months, so you are probably just going about your business as usual even now, a year on!

You are not particularly phased or stressed by the lockdowns. You have just found them tedious and feel quite indignant at the government in their handling of the lockdowns, and the pandemic in general.

You may have used the extra time to learn tarot, to start practicing wicca magic, or something else you have had your eye on but lacked the time to delve deeper into. The only problem that may occur, is if your active imagination, veering toward the apocalyptic, begins to run away with you. This is a rabbit hole that can take you to a dark place and as such, should be avoided.

As the myth buster of the zodiac, you will soon let us all know if there is any truth to the conspiracy theories bandied about on the internet.

If you are in a role that made you exempt from the lockdowns, you may have felt a little disappointed. However, you usually tend to be ok with going with the flow of life and just got stuck into the changes. That is unless they do not suit you and you feel they are a violation of your rights, then you will not take it lying down and will always fight back whenever you feel the need. They say it is the quiet ones to watch and you Scorpio, are quiet until it matters.

Feeling sick Scorpio? Makes the most of the time!

Scorpio is never afraid to take a sick day. They think temporarily disappearing from school or work adds to the mystery and intrigue of their character, and they are never going to pass up on the chance to take things easy.

When you are not feeling well, you are happy to rest at home and catch up on everything you have been missing out on. You tend to like being left alone to do your thing to get well when you are poorly.

Shut in with a Scorpio?

If you have been spending your time with a Scorpio, you will have seen how deep these souls really go. It feels like they are a bottomless pit of emotions, and have a depth to them that draws you in. Some people find this very unnerving, and you will have met sides of your Scorpio during this pandemic that you may not have known existed previously, even if you have known them your whole life!

Scorpios are mostly quiet and mysterious roommates, but you may have had some of the most intense conversations of your life during the past year. You may suddenly realise that they have you sussed, and you may have felt put under the microscope with no place to hide... Just a word of advice, Scorpio's are super intuitive and seem to know everything about you anyway, there is no fighting it so just go with the flow and bare that soul!

Missing most?

Your deep emotional connections with others that you are not able to see.

Enjoying most?

Having time to dive deep into their personal subjects of interest and into their own psyche.

Initial reaction to the virus?

Suspicion about what the media is telling people. Going on a truth-seeking mission to what is really going on in the world.

Opinion on the lockdown?

The slower pace of life suits Scorpio, but the distance from the people they love does not, and neither does being told what they can and cannot do.

Thoughts on the future?

With such a big shift in the world, life will never go back to the way it was. It is time to let the old world go and adapt to the new world as it unfolds.

Sagittarius

Sagittarius

ASTRO BABIES

The world literally is not big enough for you Sagittarius, and being confined to your home, whether an apartment or large house, can seem extremely small after a few hours, let alone weeks or months! If any sign is going to imagine the walls closing in, it is you!

To take care of all that unused energy and general enthusiasm for life during the first lockdown, you may have found a great outlet in streaming yoga classes, (with only a couple of clumsy out-takes to speak of!) or you began teaching seminars on your favourite subjects and finally had the time to share your wisdom and knowledge with the world. As the inspirational speaker of the zodiac this has been your Winston Churchill moment! Time to grab the microphone, and livestream your positive upbeat, 'everything is going to be OK' speeches, jokes, and positive affirmations just when the world needs to hear them the most.

During the second lockdown, this positivity started to wane when you realised that the travel industry was not overcoming the issues of the pandemic in 2021. Even if you did not plan to travel, the fact that it has become so difficult to do so a year after the start of the pandemic has knocked your optimism.

The key is to keep your guru hat on to compensate for the reality of your worst-case scenario: no overseas travel.

As with all of the outgoing signs of the zodiac, the potential for depression is high with you Sagittarius, so please remember to reach out for help if you feel as though you are sinking.

If you have been one of the brave key workers during this time, you will have taken all of the hype in your stride and your leadership qualities will have shone through.

You like to keep everything in life as light-hearted as possible, so your comedic value may have mixed responses depending on who you are in front of. I imagine most will welcome it though, as keeping things jolly can really lift everyone's mood.

Sagittarius got the Sniffles? Fights it for as long as possible!

For Sagittarius, getting sick is just not an option. They will do everything to reject the sickness, from taking every vitamin and medicine known to man, to pretending that everything is under control. Of course, these remedies do not work every time, and when

Sagittarius finally succumbs to getting ill, it hits them hard.

Good luck getting them to do anything, because they can be the most dependent and whiny of all the signs in this stage. They expect to be looked after well when they are sick. They want lots of sympathy and they tend to feel like their symptoms are worse than anyone else's. Good job they do not tend to get sick a lot!

Shackled with a Sagittarius?

No one person can be all and everything to a Sagittarius, and this has been your biggest challenge if you have been locked down with someone with strong Sagittarian traits. They are usually balls of enthusiastic optimism, and they love sharing their thoughts and musings with the world.

They hate any kind of confinement and can be driven mad by even they thought of having to stay in one place for an hour, let alone for months. Their tireless energy and equally crippling and maddening boredom in these special circumstances can be so draining for one person to handle, especially when it can evolve into big debates labelled 'discussions' and their argumentative side comes out to play.

Missing most?

The personal freedom to choose and travelling!

Enjoying most?

Being the voice of the masses and having time to spread your knowledge on the open forums of the world wide web!

Initial reaction to the virus?

A virus, is a virus, is a virus! I will be fine; I do not get ill.

Opinion on the lockdown?

Hate them to the core!

Thoughts on the future?

Adapt and overcome is your motto... Let us learn and retain this knowledge for the future.

Capricorn

Capricorn

ASTRO BABIES

During the first lockdown, your natural pessimism, let us call it your sense of preparedness, and an outlook permanently set on reality, will ensure that, just like Taurus and Virgo, your household is well stocked for the lockdown, you have pre-booked your online grocery shopping for the coming months, and you and your family are well sorted with all of the essentials.

If any sign is predisposed to make the most of this time, Capricorn has the business mind and tenacity to do it.

As an earth sign, you revel at the chance to start a new business, create a stay-at-home structure, and re-organise your lockdown life accordingly. You will choose the best part of the house, set up your home office, and make like the entrepreneur you were born to be, working your way to the top of the mountain and create a social architecture to stabilise your community at the same time.

By now though Capricorn, you are either flying high and cashing in on blinging masks or hand sanitiser belts, or you are struggling with the work/life balance more than ever before! Over worked is an understatement because you will not have had the boundaries that you previously had of leaving the house to go out to work. At least then you could shut the door on it for some family or you time when you got home.

If your new ventures have not been a success, you may feel quite deflated by now, and more than that, you may feel positively terrified of your financial future. Especially if your industry of work has been one of the ones that has been hit hard by the current circumstances. Try to take a deep breath, take a break from pushing yourself and find a way to de-stress. When you go back to it with fresh eyes, know that you always find a way Capricorn! That is what you are good at and now is not the time to give up!

If you have been out at work during the pandemic, you will have been relieved to have been one of the people still able to earn a living. Your work is extremely important to you and so, you will take it deadly serious.

You will feel proud to be helping others but equally humble about it. Just be careful not to take on too much Capricorn. I know that many industries have struggled with staff being off sick, but you need to ensure you do not burn yourself out and join them through shear exhaustion.

Capricorn got the coronavirus? Still manages to get everything done!

Capricorn's issue is that they put everything else ahead of their health. Unfortunately, it is not uncommon for Capricorn to be sick a lot. They run themselves into the ground because their work is always a top priority. Putting everything before their health is a habit that they have cultivated from a young age.

When they get sick, they suck it up and carry on as best as possible. They do not hide it well like Virgo, they sometimes do have to take themselves to bed, but they will take their laptop and work phone with them, so nothing falls behind. They often seem sicker and take longer to recover than everyone else because of this.

They will never expect or ask others to take care of them, even though secretly they do want to be taken care of. They are like dogs in this sense, they would rather go to a secluded place and suffer there than to allow others to see them as vulnerable and a burden.

Cooped up with a Capricorn?

If you have been locked down with your Capricorn companion, you may have been in awe at how they have handled this situation. They have dug in and got on with it probably better than any of the other signs. Although this can be inspiring and perhaps has given you the push to make the most of it too, it can be equally tiring and by now, you may be quite concerned at how hard they are being on themselves.

There has literally been no off button for work as home and work has merged into one. Perhaps you are driven mad by the lack of time they have spent with you. If you are not involved in their grand schemes, then perhaps that is a way for you to reconnect with them?

Missing most?

Work. If you cannot work, then you will not really know what to do with yourself!

Enjoying most?

The time to start your own business... If ever there was a sign that could make money out of this pandemic, it is going to be a Capricorn!

Initial reaction to the virus?

Worried about the future of the economy. That needs to be protected.

Opinion on the lockdown?

People still need to work and earn money...
But I understand it is a fine balance.

Thoughts on the future?

Grave concerns on how we are going to
recover financially as the whole economy has
taken a hit!

Aquarius

Aquarius
ASTRO BABIES

As an Aquarius, you are a social air sign, but your nature does lend you to the 'deeper intellectual work' that others often prefer to avoid, and this means you do prefer time to yourself too. For this reason, you probably feel that the universe just helped you out with a global 'do not disturb' sign hung on every door on the planet, ensuring that your train of thought is uninterrupted.

Every Aquarius has a novel, scientific discovery, or social manifesto inside them. And so, during the first lockdown you probably decided to use the time to your advantage and start a long-awaited project. Make sure to leave a trail of breadcrumbs, so you do not become lost in the vast reaches and deep space of your mind, mad scientist style!

Want the social contact, while still social distancing? Why not mirror your fellow Aquarian Oprah Winfry, and create your own talk show or podcast on your favourite subjects, no matter how 'out there' they may be, people love hearing your unique perspectives on the world. Also remember that all of your loved ones are home too at the moment, so what better time to give them a call and reconnect?!

During the second lockdown you may have become restless and as a result, your rebellious nature reared up when Christmas was cancelled. You could have gone either way with these feelings. You either decided to go full anarchist and just did what you had planned, or maybe even got involved with the anti-lockdown protests to fight for individual freedoms, as well as highlighting the damage to mental health that the isolation have caused. Or you totally went the other way and demanded that everyone follow the rules for the sake of the vulnerable in society as the humanitarian soul you are. Either way you are a justice warrior and cannot wait any longer to come out of your inner space and back into the world.

As the humanitarians of the zodiac social issues are high on your list of interest.

If you have been out there in the world as a key worker, you will have enjoyed being a part of the solution. Whatever role you are playing through the pandemic, you will easily detach from your feelings for the greater good.

You do tend to take a stance on circumstances that affect us as a collective, and depending upon what you decide, you may well be quite vocal about it, joining in with the movement for change, revolution, or whatever you think is for the common good. Just remember to pull back the reins occasionally, and to allow others their opinion too.

Aquarius under attack from Covid? - They soldier on!

Aquarius always knows how to roll with the punches, and that does not change when they get sick. They crave freedom and independence, and since feeling unwell totally cramps their style, they will do anything to avoid it.

When they feel something coming on, Aquarius simply takes preventative steps by ingesting all of the right supplements and medicines, then powers through their day. No matter how bad they feel, their determination will get them through it.

Attached to an Aquarius?

The secret to getting along with an Aquarius in any setting, is sacrificing some of your time to understand more of their pet interests. They enjoy talking about their hopes and dreams, their interests, and their specialist subjects, so if you want to get your turn to share, start by spending a couple of minutes appreciating their knowledge and words of wisdom.

An Aquarius always wants to get to the heart of that subject since they suck at small talk. Once an Aquarius feels heard, it is easier for them to move on and consider listening to others.

By now, if you have been locked up with your Aquarius friend or lover, you may have noticed that they are not the best at emotional support. For instance, if you are complaining to an Aquarius about your personal struggle with the lockdowns, they will earnestly launch into a lecture explaining all of the ways you could help yourself or use the lockdowns to your advantage - all before you get into the details let alone ask for their advice. Best practices for managing Covid, self-development, and ideas to start a business will all come at you with exuberant force, wrapped up with the best intentions. Aquarius can be completely unaware of how condescending they come across, thinking that they are being helpful by serving friends and loved ones cold, hard logic when what they really want is some emotional support.

Just hold on to the fact that they mean well and that, being innately genius in many subjects, they might well have some good advice to offer.

Missing most?

Freedom and travel... Plus the random chats you had with your co-workers and your local markets or vegan cafe!

Enjoying Most?

Having free rein to be as socially distanced as you like to be, without having to explain this to people! You can go AWOL without having to tell your nearest and dearest!

Initial reaction to the virus?

What can I do to help? Stay away from other people? Cool! A fair few Aquarians will be in the conspiracy club as they are naturally suspicious.

Opinion on the lockdown?

Fine by me, so long as I can do my thing it's fine... I cannot do what now? Try and stop me!

Thoughts on the future?

People should have the right to choose. End of! Or the opposite... People need to suck it up and do the right thing to help the most vulnerable in society.

Pisces

Pisces

ASTRO BABIES

Pisces, finally you have time to float, dream, and manifest your creative oeuvre. With nowhere you need to be, you can dive down into your big vision and start to make some progress on making it happen. Either you make your biggest wish come true, or you while away the days writing a dream journal, plunging deeper into your unconscious through your meditation and yoga practice, or simply catching up on some much-needed self-care. Now that you have your days free to indulge yourself you feel totally chill.

You can, however, be prone to an overactive imagination, which can lead to hypochondriac tendencies, so it is important to focus on a project to keep the hypochondria at bay.

One thing to keep an eye on is any bad habits that might creep in, especially during this latest lockdown. Alcohol and drugs are not your friend, especially if you are feeling lonely, fed up, or sad about the state of the world. It can be easy for you to slip into feeling a deep empathy for friends and family that have been going through a hard time for the past year, and you may want to numb that overwhelming sea of emotion with drugs, alcohol, or chocolate.

Instead try having a nice relaxing bath with calming essential oils, watch a fun movie that makes you laugh out loud, meditate, or get lost in a good book.

Remember that it is ok to feel, and it is best to try and acknowledge and work through your feelings as and when they come up as opposed to hiding from them. For this reason, Pisces, consider getting some counselling to help you deal with the changes that are happening within the world and to help you cope.

It makes sense that many compassionate Pisces folk are within caring roles, such as nursing or taking care of the elderly. I imagine that the past year has been extremely difficult for you to deal with because you are tuned into the energies and emotions of others.

Being within your role, whatever it may be, is usually tough, but the pandemic has probably sent you into overdrive. Therefore, you have to be careful not to make yourself sick with worry and getting lost in empathising with what everyone around you is feeling.

Pisces feeling peaky? Just sleeps!

Pisces does not have time for feeling icky. When they catch something, they know that the best remedy is fluids and rest. Self-care is their top priority, and they are happy to sleep for days on end if it means that they will feel good as new at the end of it. Everything else can wait until they feel better.

Just be aware that because they sometimes find keeping boundaries difficult, it can help to remind them that they are entitled to put their needs first and to say no to the demands of others.

Penned in with a Pisces?

While people who are not fellow water signs, consider Pisces an emotional wreck for getting weepy over every little thing… This may be the furthest thing from the truth. They are usually totally fine, but just love a good cry from time to time.

Before the lockdowns, you knew that your Pisces friend, family member, or lover was a sensitive soul. Now that you have been with them all day, every day for the past year, it may have dawned on you that there is actually, no end to their deep ocean of moods, emotions, and feelings.

You may have had to pull them back from the brink of borderline addictive behaviours from time to time, (not all Pisces of course) but mainly, you will have witnessed how utterly compassionate they can be in your time of need. Not to mention that they are a soft, calming rock for anyone who reaches out for help. This has left you with a new perspective on your lovable friend. You realise that they absorb and hold the emotions of the world, at least their small section of it, and this is a far cry from the emotional wreck that you thought you knew.

Pisces are strong and do what they need to do to carry the weight of the burden they hold within their soul.

Missing most?

Not much. Just the freedom to walk around without a mask and without the fear of the virus might be nice.

Enjoying most?

Reconnecting to yourself, having the pressure from society removed so you can do your thing.

Initial reaction to the virus?

You probably felt the whole world gasp and stress about it. It took you a while to process all of that fear emotion, and you wanted to just go to bed and hide.

Opinion on the lockdown?

You secretly wish life is always like this even though you hate that some people are having a rough time.

Thoughts on the future?

You hope that the sense of community and love for one another holds true into the future.

Part 2:

The Astrology of

2020

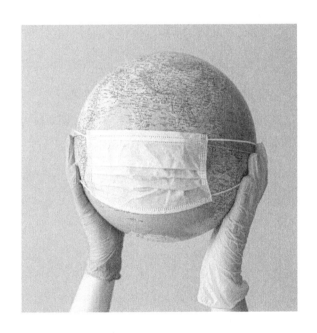

Now we understand more of what our personal reactions have been to this situation, lets zoom out to explore how the world at large is affected, and what is going on in the astrological weather that has created such a catastrophic couple of years.

So, why has this happened in the first place you might ask? There are many factors to consider, but there are a couple of specific astrological transits that can explain the events that have transpired within the last year. Below is an overview of the main factors based on the past year's astrology transits, as well as the main transits of this coming year and how they are affecting us all as a collective and individually.

As I look back at the events of the past year in the UK, as well as the rest of the world, we sit in lockdown, or a state of uneasiness, there seems to be a mixture of feelings in the air. Therefore, I want to use my astrological knowledge to help you make a little more sense of it all. From stress and fear to a new sense of community and unity, plus some confusion and conspiracy floating around too, it has been quite the roller coaster ride.

At present, the government here in the UK have not given us an end date to this quarantine, and just a basic idea on their strategy to get the country back up and running. Some say it may be a repeat of 2020 where we have some respite during the summer months, and things may begin to close down again in the autumn. Some predict that we will never really go back to the way things were in the past.

When the world feels crazy and we are faced with an uncertain future, we all want to find answers and predictions for what is potentially coming next. The ancient art of astrology can definitely help us to see through the fog right now.

Predictive astrologers have anticipated this kind of worldwide event for many years, but how did they know that this was coming?

Below are some of the transits that have occurred, how they relate to what has transpired, and the upcoming transits that can give us some idea on what course this is likely to take over the next year or so.

Pluto and Saturn in Capricorn

From international travel restrictions, to shaken financial markets, and a virus yet to be contained, astrologers have known for many years that an economic downturn and huge disruptions would be triggered by the Saturn-Pluto conjunction in Capricorn on January 12th, 2020. This particular conjunction has been building since 2018 and, at its finale, it has created waves throughout the world. Capricorn is where this conjunction was set and this is the sign that rules governments, the economy, and work in general.

Saturn is the ruler of Capricorn, and so it was in its home sign during the conjunction, giving the events that developed over the past year extra punch. Saturn also represents building things up the 'right' way, foundations, old age, time, karma, traditions, keeping the status quo, and restriction.

Pluto on the other hand, is the planet of death (metaphorically and physically, as well as mental or societal) destruction, rebirth and the hidden or dark elements of our universe, things that we cannot see, including viruses and bacteria. This makes Pluto and Saturn (along with Mars) the great malefic planets of our solar system.

Pluto wants to tear down what is already here, the old worn-out ways of the past. It can be destructive, turning the world upside down, and then just as suddenly it becomes beautiful as it transforms into something new and refreshed, like a phoenix rising from the ashes.

Saturn represents structure, the old, government, rules, regulations, laws, restriction, and karma. Saturn is hard-nosed, cold, and calculated. Transits that involve Saturn are harsh, and you often must endure hard work, restrictions, and often painful learning experiences before you see rewards for your efforts.

What Happened Last Time This Conjunction Happened in Capricorn?

To explore the effects of this conjunction further, we can look back in history to make comparisons with what happened then, to what is happening now. To understand the present, it always helps to understand the past.

These two planets conjoined in Capricorn for the first time in 1518, and during this time, although not as prevalent as today's pandemic (more on this shortly), there was a mysterious dancing plague that swept across Europe.

People who contracted the 'disease', began dancing involuntarily, and were unable to stop! They dropped down of exhaustion and many died.

Around the year of 1518, there was significant upheaval as we moved out of the dark ages at the end of the 1400's, into the post-medieval period and slowly toward the renaissance period, which literally translates as rebirth (Pluto).

In 1518 moving through to 1520, Martin Luther challenged Pope Leo X because of the exploitation of the common people by the church, whereby they were charging money for the chance to not only resolve their sins of the past, but also settle sins they had planned for the future. These were called 'indulgences' (another link to Pluto) and only the clergy could atone you. You were even told that your deceased loved ones would be left eternally in purgatory unless you paid to absolve the sins they collected during their lifetime. It was a complete and utter scam of the highest order, and the core motive was monetary gain. The selling of indulgences is still a cause of embarrassment for the Catholic church to this day.

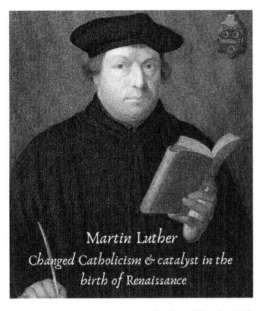

Martin Luther

Changed Catholicism & catalyst in the birth of Renaissance

Does any of this sound familiar? When indulgences began to be peddled in Germany, Martin Luther wrote a thesis in protest. As he was an ordained priest, his opinion held weight and demanded attention unlike the many complaints of the common people before him. His influence only grew as the years passed and as his views became more extreme, they became more at odds with the

Catholic Church than he originally intended them to be, as he did not set out to challenge the overarching power of the Catholic Church. Initially, he did not even see his views as diverging from principle.

However, in the few months between Luther drafting his theses in 1517 and the Saturn-Pluto conjunction in 1518, (and beyond that) the Catholic Church made the Protestant Reformation all but inevitable through their reluctance to reform.

As the Reformation gained momentum through the 16th century, this foundation completely challenged how the Catholic Church consolidated its influence.

Reformers also called for the widespread availability of local translations (i.e. not in Latin) of the Scriptures. This was the move towards people gaining more knowledge and the evolution of the people.

As the conjunction began to build, Martin Luther and his followers demanded change. Luther's theses, entitled Ninety-five Theses or Disputation on the Power and Efficacy of Indulgences was literally nailed to the church doors at the end of 1517. This was a momentous shift towards truth.

The Catholic Church as an institution was consumed with "a deep-rooted corruption" as historian Ludwig Pastor put it, and under the influence of Pluto it was made even more glaringly obvious; the rot within the system was exaggerated and unavoidable. Anyone could see change was coming.

At this point in history, the Vatican's authority was nigh unquestionable, (very Saturn) and Christianity was the bedrock of

Western society and culture (therein lies Capricorn's influence). Yet even at the height of the excesses of the time, those in charge were facing a moment of accountability. You will not be surprised to learn that despite growing anger from most of the population, church leaders decided to bury their heads in the sand, believing the power of the church would never be diluted.

No action was taken and by the time the conjunction rolled around in January 1518, events were set into motion that all but solidified the death of that system and its supremacy.

A complete examination of the effects of the Reformation is beyond the scope of this work, but it is, suffice to say, that Western society changed irrevocably. The Europe we see today is largely the result of the protestant reformation and the events of 1518 and beyond.

There was an indirect backlash against the pomposity and grandiosity of Rome through iconoclasm, (the rejection and destruction of visual images which happened originally when the Roman empire converted to Christianity, and which the Renaissance had just worked so hard to restore), and the cataclysmic Sack of Rome in 1527; something utterly unfathomable before the 1518 conjunction. After all, who could ever imagine violent mobs running amok and destroying the sacred institutions of state in the capital city of a nation?

Over time, the splintering of Christianity, and specifically the Catholic church caused its power and political influence to wane, setting the stage for The Enlightenment, which eventually translated into the events we are living today.

Standing in our moment, and in light of the previous conjunction in Capricorn, we are not that far removed from 1518. Some might almost suggest we are due a second reformation, and another Enlightenment (The Age of Aquarius comes to mind!), when we look back at the last few decades and the events that have brought us to this place.

Where we are going, today, and what our recent Saturn-Pluto conjunction will mean is still largely unknown, and dependent upon our choices now. The similarities between the conjunction of 1518 and todays are more than obvious, but it will still be useful to explore them further. Saturn and Pluto meet every 33-35 years, but in a different zodiac sign, taking nearly three centuries to return to a sign.

Other interesting effects of past Pluto and Saturn conjunctions...

The last Pluto-Saturn conjunction on November 8th, 1982, coincided with the end of a brief recession. The world economy remained in the doldrums throughout 1982 and high unemployment affected OECD nations until at least 1985.

Historically, there have been incidences of economic shakeups or wars whenever these two planets unite. The cluster of Saturn-Pluto unions of 1914-15 merged with the start of World War I and the effects stretched until the next Saturn-Pluto conjunction (in Leo) in 1947, which aligned with the end of World War II.

On November 16th, 1914, the U.S. Federal Reserve began operations as Saturn and Pluto (both retrograde) conjunct in Cancer.

Right before that, the world was rocked by the Financial Panic of 1914. With impending war threatening global markets, alarmed investors pulled out of their securities in a rush for cash and gold. This led to an unparalleled shutdown of the London Stock Exchange for five months, and the U.S. Stock Exchange for four months.

Even more shockingly, for six weeks during August and early September 1914 (as Saturn and Pluto made close contact) almost every stock exchange in the world was closed.

So, What Happened in 2020?

This look into the previous conjunction certainly gives us in insight to the world we are moving into now. Parallels show that in the face of complete and utter abuse of power (Pluto) and responsibility (Saturn) on the part of the institutions (Capricorn) accountable for tending to the needs of the common people, citizens begin to cry out for reform.

The breakdown of the old, outdated traditions where Pluto conjuncts Saturn in Capricorn, appears to be a catalyst for a fight towards the destruction of Capricorn's institutions, which eventually brings a rebirth of a new world (Pluto's transformation, and The Age of Aquarius) and a slow and decisive rebuilding of new structures to support society in a better way (Saturn and Jupiter in Aquarius).

Hence, the most recent meeting of Pluto and Saturn in Capricorn began in 2018 and has been increasing in intensity during that time. They have been traveling in close contact from December 2019, making an exact conjunction on January 13th, 2020 and continuing to move together through to late February 2020. One day beforehand, the first person died of the virus in China, and during the following several days, the virus began to spread throughout the world.

Before we delve into the affects this conjunction has had on our health and well-being I.e., the virus, the global economy has also succumbed to the ever-present dangers of economic deterioration.

This has set the stage for the ultimate Plutonian story, a random event that has occurred outside of the parameters of statistical modelling and status quo perspectives and delivered us with a surprise beyond anything that we could have ever imagined.

At the point of the conjunction and the threat of the virus becoming a global pandemic, the U.S stock market took a steep plunge due to virus-induced fears and developments.

Markets from Europe to Brazil and Asia were rattled by concerns about the coronavirus economic impact.

In China, we witnessed the core of global manufacturing crumble and lose tens of billions of pounds in growth within the first few months, because of the coronavirus shutdowns.

Warnings were also made that major outbreaks in Japan, South Korea and Italy underscore the risk posed to other big economies from the coronavirus.

With the Covid-19 virus spreading at the rate it did, it became a certainty that it would affect every nation and their economies as the disrupted global supply chain began exporting in panic.

The UK was already set to lose its trade deals with the EU after pushing Brexit through at the end of 2019. Despite the added blow to the economy, because of the pandemic ensuring near collapse for many industries, and a myriad of warnings from economists and financial experts, the British government pushed ahead and left the EU officially at the end of 2020.

For the UK this will be a devastating fall into recession and has parallels to the 1518 conjunction and its catalytic mechanism for the eventual collapse of the catholic church. The working class will suffer the most because of this huge historical event, yet those in charge, the powerful and wealthy, have managed to convince the people to vote for something that will essentially lock them into a deep and damaging recession, where the rich have already taken advantage, and profited from the spoils.

Many people have woken up to what has happened, and there is already a feeling of revolution and demand for change in the air.

In a similar way, we will likely see change in the coming years. This may come in the way countries are governed, as opposed to the reformation of a religious kind, and there are predictions of a potential rebuilding of these establishments in the future and during the age of Aquarius.

Back to the virus itself... The difference between 1518 and its dancing plague, and the current novel coronavirus, is that not only did we have Pluto and Saturn conjunct in Capricorn, but this time around, Jupiter also joined Pluto in conjunction in March 2020.

Jupiter's influence in 2020

If there is one aspect that is directly 'responsible' for Covid-19 becoming a worldwide pandemic, it is the Pluto/Jupiter conjunction. The first case of the Covid-19 virus was detected as Jupiter entered Capricorn. On December 1st, 2019, the very first case was detected in Wuhan, China. This occurred as Jupiter, the planet of international travel and exchange, was preparing to end a 13-month stay in its home sign of Sagittarius.

On December 2nd, Jupiter moved into its fall position in Capricorn, joining Saturn and Pluto in this sobering sign and it seems the effect of Jupiter's presence acted like a release on things that were kept suppressed, including the virus.

The Jupiter and Pluto Conjunction

The Pluto and Jupiter conjunction in Capricorn that happened on March 21st - April 5th, 2020, and as previously mentioned, Pluto rules pandemics and the major life and death cycles, while Jupiter rules societal issues and has a quality of spreading and magnifying everything it touches.

Both Jupiter and Pluto have an amplifying quality, and when they join, they tend to blow things out of proportion.

Usually, Jupiter has a benefic character and when you find it gracing a house within your chart, you are generally pleased with the changes that it bestows upon you.

After the conjunction at the end of March, the UK announced its first lockdown, closing schools and 'non-essential' shops, public places, and events, as well as urging the general public to stay home, and not see family and friends until further notice.

In Italy, there were stories in the media of hospitals being overrun with cases and the country as a whole was shut down. The travel industry was also devastated by the restrictions and we had entered into a world that nobody saw coming.

This was also around the time of Saturn moving into Aquarius and so restrictions were amplified more than ever before. Just remembering back to March 18th, 2020, and what was occurring at the time of this stellium, (there were actually six planets within the sign of Capricorn, five of which were in a tight conjunction) the world literally exploded with news of the pandemic and Covid-19.

In much of Europe, it was the same story, give or take a week, and worldwide, people everywhere were reacting to the virus.

The period between March 18th and March 23rd, Mars had a hand to play in the conjunction with Pluto and hence this small period of time was particularly problematic. This increased that of a more aggressive approach to control people's movements.

Just to return to the point of Jupiter and Pluto once more... This conjunction does happen every 13 years, and of course this does not mean we will have a virus or a pandemic every 13 years. But because Jupiter and Pluto are part of this previously mentioned larger stellium in Capricorn, and as earth signs have much more tangibility, the influence brought to the planet at this time is much more powerful.

Side note: Because the conjunction happened in Capricorn, a sign associated with old age, this correlates to the elderly population being more affected by the virus.

North and South Nodes Square Chiron

Another transit that got overlooked is the Nodes square Chiron. The Nodes of the Moon are also connected to viruses in astrology.

During the initial part of the pandemic, we had the South Node in Capricorn and the North Node in Cancer, the opposing sign of Capricorn. Chiron, also known as 'the wounded healer', is in Aries.

The Nodes-Chiron square started to form early in 2020 and peaked in mid-March. Chiron, although not directly connected to viruses, certainly increased the feelings of vulnerability, fear, and helplessness around this time.

The Nodes square Chiron suggest that we are at a karmic crossroads and indicate that it is a time to discover how to embrace our vulnerability in times of ambiguity.

In May 2020, the nodes shifted signs into Gemini North Node and Sagittarius South Node. This did seem to add to the shift in energy as people began to 'settle in' to their locked down way of life. I imagine that the nice weather helped, and cases of the virus began to lessen as the summer wore on.

People began seeking out online courses to keep their mind occupied. Schools set up e-learning models for schooling children from home, and people got used to working from a home office too.

Video calling apps, such as Zoom, literally zoomed into a billion-pound company. Let's face it, 2020 was the year to get online and start making money any way you can, and this is only going to become truer as we move forward into Aquarius!

From Capricorn to Aquarius

After Pluto played its part, the faster moving planets moved on into Aquarius, leaving Pluto in Capricorn until March 2023. It is important to keep in mind that Pluto's higher purpose is to make us more resilient, so that we stand a better chance of survival in the future. We all need to take responsibility for what is going on in the world right now and learn our lessons to take forward into the coming Age of Aquarius.

Have we stagnated? Got too complacent?

An example of this is the way we produce our food. Although there are a few theories about where the virus originated from, the idea that it came from a wet market in Wuhan is not too difficult to comprehend. There is a myriad of animals, kept at these markets in small cages, in close proximity, and in unsanitary conditions.

The story is the same all over the globe, and this practice is not only barbaric, but also poses a threat to humanity. A plethora of pathogens all mingling together is a hotbed for developing novel bacteria and viruses and this is not the first time that this has happened.

Swine flu originated from a pig farm in the USA, and Ebola was born out of Africa from 'bush meat'.

In fact, according to the CDC "every pandemic over the past one hundred years, has arisen as a direct consequence of inhuman treatment of animals for meat production and consumption." Therefore, it goes without saying that meat production and animal welfare is a global issue that needs a total reform if this is to be prevented in the future.

Pluto is here to remind us that change is a constant of life, and to embrace it every step of the way. If we as a collective take note of this fact, then there is a lesser chance for things like this pandemic to happen in the future.

Saturn Enters Aquarius and Conjuncts Jupiter

After the conjunction to Pluto in January 2020, Saturn moved on from Pluto and through Capricorn, finally entering Aquarius for the first time on 21st March. This marked the first point of a three-year journey into the Age of Aquarius, an air sign, indicative of some challenges that come in the form of anything that is spread through the atmosphere, including respiratory infections and airborne diseases.

As restrictive Saturn entered the sign that rules society and community, including all group gatherings, this phase evidently impacted on community and social services. We will likely see Saturn's imprint on public health and government-operated offices under Aquarian rule, with delays and bureaucracy.

With Saturn's tendency to be extra cautious, people tend to become more divided, and this shows where the inclination for quarantining and shutdowns of many hospitality businesses, came in as a solution to containing the virus. Saturn in social Aquarius brought about the cancellation of events, holidays, and conferences in March through to July and then again in December 2020.

As well as this we saw a divide in many groups of people. Black Lives Matter being one example and the increasing tension leading up to the election in America between Trump supporters and Biden supporters.

There is always some division between people in these matters, however, with the

Saturn/Jupiter conjunction in Aquarius, it was certainly intensified and there were more protests and anarchistic groups forming. This is going to be ever more prevalent as we move further into the age of Aquarius.

We also saw a shortage of face masks, Personal protective equipment and some medicines since China produces much of the world's supply. Mars followed not long after, on April 1st, 2020.

Here the mood shifted towards the impact of freedom of movement of the people. In many ways, Saturn moving into Aquarius and away from Pluto released the tension and heaviness that we all felt during the earlier conjunctions.

We sought new connections with each other through online groups, events, and support systems. However, the quarantine areas began to spread, and not long after this event, air travel restrictions were put into place. (Aquarius is the sign of air travel).

The Jupiter/Saturn conjunction was one of the longest Astrological transits we saw in 2020 as it concluded on December 21st, with what I liked to call 'the wild conjunction'.

On a positive note, after the heaviness of Earth and Capricorn energy, we all buckled down, and a community spirit arose in many people.

We began exploring new ways of doing things, mainly related to people or places. Perhaps you started an online course, wanted to learn something that was going to improve your career and work prospects, or just to keep your mind occupied.

With Saturn in Aquarius however, a number of responsibilities might have knocked at your door. This could have been working from home, home schooling your children, and if you were working in key worker positions, then I can only imagine the responsibility you must have felt during this time. This was definitely intensified when the nodes shifted in May.

On April 7th, 2020 Mars and Saturn both also squared Uranus in Taurus. This is the first of many squares to come over 2021, and these squares will be the beginning of many sudden changes and events during this coming year.

Just as an example, Uranus being the planet of sudden and unexpected events, really took the UK by surprise as our Prime Minister Boris Johnson, was admitted to hospital with the coronavirus within a few days of this transit.

Jupiter in Aquarius

When Jupiter entered Aquarius for the final time after 12 years. We all had high hopes for the future. Jupiter in Aquarius is about looking forward, thinking big, and embracing the new face of humanity.

However, on December 21st, the wild conjunction of Jupiter and Saturn occurred at 0 degrees. Both Jupiter and Saturn are vastly different planets, and when they met it was always going to be a catalyst for massive change and disruption in our lives for several reasons.

This triggered the last-minute lockdown right before Christmas here in the UK, and a resurgence of the virus. I think most people had really pinned their hopes on being with the people they loved at the end of the year.

Then restrictive Saturn put the brakes on yet again.

Having this conjunction right at the end of 2020 really summed up everything that 2020 was! So, what does that mean for 2021?

Part 3:

2021
and the saga
continues!

After the events of 2020, we were all hoping that we would wake up in 2021 with a fresh new world. I think this feeling came as a result of the shift of energy from Capricorn and into Aquarius at the end of 2020. However, it felt as though nothing had really moved forward.

In the UK we were still in lockdown, after the Saturn and Jupiter conjunction in Aquarius, where there was a hope that this would bring freedom from Saturn's restrictions. Yet this did not occur due to the fact that Saturn is a stronger force than Jupiter when in Aquarius.

However, what did happen was a rapid scientific breakthrough with various new vaccines ready for use. This new technology could be interpreted as both a positive and negative step, depending on what side of the fence you sit on with this issue. There was also a sudden surge of variants and more cases of the virus at the point of the conjunction and a swift return into lockdown in the UK, just in time for Christmas and New Year and this is still continuing on the anniversary on our first lockdown.

As previously mentioned, Jupiter's symbolism is not only about freedom and hope, but also growth and so when Saturn united with Jupiter, it expanded the restrictive nature of Saturn. For this reason, during 2021, Jupiter will do much better once it has escaped from Saturn. We will then see more expansion and freedom in our world.

January was a tough month overall. On January 6th, 2021, a mob of Trump supporters launched an attack on the Capitol in Washington as Pluto conjunct Mercury in Capricorn, and squared Mars in Gemini. As we know, Pluto is revolution, and Mars is the planet of war, action, and aggression. Mercury is the planet of communication and communicate their dissatisfaction they did!

On January 20th, 2021, Mars was in conjunction Uranus. This changed the course of history with Joe Biden inaugurated as the President of the USA as the oldest person ever inaugurated at 78, and Kamala Harris becoming the first female Vice President of the United States.

When does Jupiter move away from Saturn?

As I write this, March 20th, 2021, Jupiter is 10 degrees away from Saturn. In fact, just as Jupiter reached 8 degrees away from Saturn on February 26, 2021, the UK presented its 'timeline to freedom' (how fitting!) and within it, the key dates leading us out of the lockdown situation in four stages, that all coincide with Jupiter's movements this year. It appears that Jupiter holds the key to our freedom of movement and is the planet to keep a close eye on.

As an example, here are the dates of the 4 stages that England have set out with a few examples:

Step 1: March 8th, 2021 – School's return (Jupiter rules education). Jupiter is now more than 8 degrees separating away from Saturn.

Step 2: April 12th, 2021 – Hospitality venues can open outdoors (Jupiter's the jovial planet in the sign of social gatherings, Aquarius).
This is also the date of the New Moon at 22 degrees Aries, a symbol of new beginnings and Jupiter will be sextile this New Moon at 26 Aquarius.

Step 3: May 17th, 2021 – Most social contact rules are being lifted, entertainment is reinstated, although with restrictions.
This is a significant shift because on May 14, 2021, Jupiter enters Pisces and remains here until July 28th, 2021. This was always going to be a positive shift for the Arts and religious ceremonies.

Step 4: June 21st, 2021 – Travel opens up on the day of the Solstice, which is an auspicious date in astrology when the Sun is at its brightest in the northern hemisphere. (Jupiter rules travel and Jupiter's transit through Pisces looks like a window of opportunity for the re-opening of travel).

Plus, Jupiter switches becomes retrograde on June 20th, 2021, again emphasising the significance of this key planet close to all four dates.

As a side note: There is already talk that the May date, when Jupiter is in Pisces will speed up the unlocking of restrictions!

Looking Ahead

Jupiter moves in a retrograde cycle back into Aquarius from July 28th to December 29th, 2021, so we may see more restrictions later this year, when Jupiter joins Saturn in this sign once more. However, Jupiter does not return to conjunct with Saturn, and so the impact will not be as dramatic as the it was at the end of 2020. In December 2021, Jupiter returns to Pisces, hopefully bestowing us with more of its good fortune.

Saturn in Aquarius

Saturn is staying put for the next three years, until March 2023, and as Saturn rules laws, rules, and regulations and Aquarius rules innovation, including anything chemical or pharmaceutical there could be some changes in these areas.

The last time Saturn was in technological Aquarius was in 1994, which was around the time the world wide web was invented and started to really take off. From that moment on, humanity has made a lot of technological advancements, so astrologers are expecting this next 27-year cycle that is about to begin to be even more meaningful when it comes to technology, medicine, and innovation in general. The Aquarian energy is also humanistic and socialist, so this transit means that activism is here to stay.

Saturn's quick dip into Aquarius in 2020 was at the height of the social justice movement that occurred during the summer. Protesters marched for George Floyd, Ahmaud Arbery, Breonna Taylor, and other victims of police brutality giving us an insight of more to come. Namely, meaningful action and activism that helps to enact the change we need in the world. But this can only happen if we actually take action!

During this time, we can expect progressive changes to transform our world, but only if we are ready to do the work and evolve with this transit. Saturn is a planet that rewards those who put in the effort, which means that what you put in you get back. If we implement growth in our lives, then we will receive gifts from the universe that will better our lives.

Uranus in Taurus

The ruling planet of Aquarius, Uranus, is in financially astute Taurus until 2026, which increase this effect. We may also see more government cover-ups, as Saturn descends on the sign that rules public information and technology. This could fan the flames of the uprisings associated with Uranus and Aquarius, especially as people demand access to information that has a direct bearing on their daily lives.

Passions about social justice, Black Lives Matter, climate change, and other pressing human rights issues, kick-started into overdrive during this transit. If there is anything we have learnt from Saturn's previous time in Aquarius, it is that we are stronger together, and we can make things happen if we join together for the greater good.

During this Saturn period people are looking to discover their own place within the collective and with Saturn in this sign, the collective will make their voices heard.

Along with this revolutionary push, we will likely see some advancements in technology, including air and spacecraft, the internet, electronic and medical technologies. Even science and academics, could begin to combine with a religion and spirituality like never before.

If there is one thing to take away from this transit, it is all about radical change, both in our world and in our personal lives. But no meaningful change can happen without actions to back it up.

So, what else do we have in store? Crypto currency could make way for a new way of handling money. As more industries are impacted by the coronavirus, we may see an acceleration in the development of bitcoin or a whole new economy altogether. This likelihood is increased thanks to radial changemaker Uranus and its eight-year revolution through Taurus, the sign that represents money and finance as well as Pluto forging through Capricorn until 2024, which might accelerate developments or alternatives for new money models over the next four years.

There is also the climate crisis that has been in the forefront of our minds over the past few years. It was brought back into our awareness by Greta Thunberg as she began her campaign in August 2018, just as Uranus in Taurus began its retrograde from Taurus back into Aries for the final time. Greta has been a pioneer for Global change, calling for the leaders of the world to stand up and make changes toward sustainability in many areas. She has inspired both love and passion, as well as an aggressive hate campaign against her for her activism work.

With indie-spirited Uranus in hardworking Taurus, the self-employed economy will grow even bigger. More people will work remotely and in co-working spaces, and the full-time employment model will continue to go extinct. Uranus in sensible and profit-driven Taurus, can help us monetize our creations in interesting new ways.

Saturn and Jupiter in Aquarius, squaring Uranus in Taurus

As I have previously mentioned this transit happens three times throughout 2021. Because of the immensity of the influence on us all this year, this is not something that happens three times and disappears in between. We will feel them subtly every day during 2021 because they are moving together and staying within a few degrees of each other throughout the entire year and into next year too.

However, this is not something that happens immediately either! Even though you may not see sudden change on the dates of these conjunctions, you can be sure that there is a massive rewiring going on in the background. Both in your personal life, and globally. The slow-moving planetary transits are slow...

and the transformation they bring takes time, it is subtle, and not very obvious.

You may not be aware of the things in your life and inside of you that change right now, but you can bet that there is a massive rewiring going on, in the background.

In February, June, and December 2021 the themes of the Saturn-Uranus square will become clearer, but keep in mind that this is an ongoing process.

Saturn and Uranus could not be more different; however, the paradox is that they work well together.

If we look at the order of planets in our solar system, Uranus follows Saturn, so there is a continuity theme there. Once the Saturn work is done, Uranus is the one that takes over from Saturn.

Uranus comes with the promise of freedom and enlightenment.

But the path to freedom and enlightenment goes through Saturn. We may all be free conscious beings by design, but we are simply not aware of this until, we first master Saturn.

Saturn and Uranus have opposite functions. Saturn creates structures. Uranus beaks these structures so that a new, superior order can emerge.

Uranus' energy is unpredictable and electrifying, stirring things up and creating excitement and restlessness.

A square is a dynamic 90-degree aspect where confrontation and change are imminent. The planets in square share the same modality (in our case, the Fixed modality).

However, they see things from completely different lenses: Uranus through the grounding, earthy Taurus lens, and Saturn through the intellectual, freedom-seeking Aquarius lens.

The clash of these 2 titans can produce extreme tension and crisis in our society and impact our lives as individuals either directly or indirectly.

Both Taurus and Aquarius are fixed signs. They do not rush like Cardinal signs do, moving to the next exciting thing, if their efforts do not pay off immediately, nor do they adapt to circumstances like mutable signs do.

They do the work, no matter how long it takes. The changes the Saturn-Uranus square will bring, will be long-lasting and will impact our society – and us, individuals in a profound way.

How have the transits affected you?

When you are examining these transits on an individual level, you first need to create your chart and find your Rising sign. To do this, you need to know your time and place of birth, in addition to your date and year of birth.

As previously mentioned, there are many free chart generator sites, but I tend to use Astro.com as you can also add the transits onto the chart to see where they are in relation to your planets and houses.

Once you have produced your chart, read on below to understand what each house represents and what each of the major transits will mean for us on a personal level.

This which will help you understand better how the transits might have affected you.

Houses

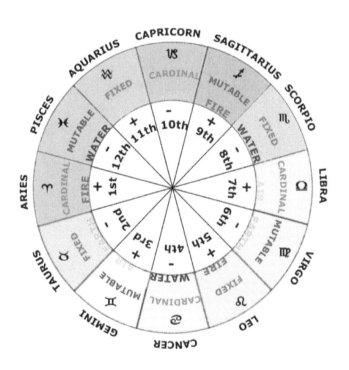

1st House

The First House is ruled by Aries and the planet Mars. It represents your image and the mask that you show to the world. It is how people see you when they meet you. It is our physical self and the way we look externally.

The first house sets off the whole chart and when a planet transits here it is easy to see in how you feel in new situations and show up in the world. You could start something new or meet new people.

2nd House

The second house is where we see our relationship with our money and earthly possessions, our self-worth and esteem.

Taurus and Venus are the house rulers and when a planet transits this house, our physical possessions are affected. We could either receive more or less money depending on the transit. This could also affect our self-esteem and how we feel about ourselves.

3rd House

The third house covers many aspects of our lives. It is ruled by Gemini and Mercury and so shows our communication style, represents school and learning, our siblings, and the relationship to them. Neighbours and acquaintances as well as our short distance travel and even our car.

When a planet transits this house, it could disrupt our travel arrangements, mean that communication is affected, or it might manifest within our local neighbourhood depending upon the planet moving through.

4th House

This house is the home of Cancer and the Moon. Therefore, it represents your home as well as what you need to feel secure and safe. It is the symbol of the way you see your mother or main caregiver as you are growing up, and as you get older, it represents your family and the roots you have created.

If a planet transits through this house, you could have issues or feelings come up around your core family environment, or something about your roots could be highlighted for you. Another thing that can happen during transits in the fourth house is that you literally move house, things are delayed if you want to move home, or simply that you change something around your current home.

5th House

The fifth house is ruled by Leo and home to the Sun. Therefore, it represents what you like to do for fun, creativity, and pleasure. It also deals with children, mainly your firstborn child, your dating life and non-committed relationships, any kind of art or business projects and anything that you create.

When a planet transits this house, you can either feel more or less creative, depending upon the transit in question. It can affect your children and your dating relationships in general. You could meet someone or end a relationship for example.

6th House

The sixth house is home to Virgo and so it is another mercury house. Here though, we are dealing with our day- to-day lives. This includes our daily habits, good deeds and service to others, small animals that are pets we keep in our own environment, our health. It also pertains to our jobs and daily work, although not our long-term careers.

When a transiting planet moves through this house, it can shake up our daily lives! Our health can improve or suffer, we can lose or gain a job, and our pets can be affected. It can also mean something as simple such as we decide to start a new workout routine.

7th House

The seventh house is another Venus house, but this time Libra is queen, is the house that rules other people in our lives. It is the way we view others in the world and how we see self through others. Here we find our long-term partners, marriage, or business, and it also shows where our competitors are. It is usually the opposite sign to your first house, hence why you can feel so attracted to people who seem so opposite to you initially.

When a transit happens here, we can see people getting married, having issues in a current long-term relationship, form new ventures with a business partner. Anything that you can see happening around your close intimate, or business relationships is usually because of a transit here.

8th House

Scorpio and Pluto rule the eighth house; hence this is the house that rules death and rebirth. It also rules sex and intimacy and how we feel about being close to those we love. It depicts how we deal with the big changes that inevitably happen in our lives. And lastly, the eighth house represents other people's money and possessions, inheritance for example.

And so, when a planet transits through your eighth house, you could lose someone and receive an inheritance, you could become more or less intimate with a partner, you could also go through your own metaphorical death and rebirth depending on the planet moving through the house and any aspects that may be hitting it.

9th House

The ninth house is ruled by Sagittarius and Jupiter. It is the house of the higher mind, spirituality, and religious themes. It represents how the external beliefs that you have been bought up with have impacted you. It also manifests as travel and other cultures as well as higher learning, such as university or adult courses.

If you have transiting planets here, they speak to all of these themes. You could travel abroad, embark upon a higher learning course or degree, or become more interested in spiritual or religious practices.

10th House

The tenth house is ruled by Saturn and Capricorn and so speaks to your reputation and what you might form a career out of.

When a transit happens here your career and what you are working towards doing in your life to fulfil any kind of meaningful work will be affected.

11th House

The Eleventh house is ruled by Aquarius and the planet Uranus. This house is the place where you find your friends and peer groups as well as your goals and aspirations. It is where your hopes and dreams are kept.

When we have positive transits moving through our eleventh house, our dreams could literally come true! Other themes could be around friends and social groups.

12th House

The twelfth house is home to Pisces and Neptune. The main themes here are sleep and dreams states, fantasies, drugs and alcohol abuse, institutions such as schools, hospitals, and prisons. It is where the deep well of the unconscious mind and processes reside.

When we have planets transiting our twelfth house, much of what these bring can be on the fringes of our life and we might not realise what is going on. In the extreme, it can mean spending some time in hospital or other institution where you have not consciously chosen to be. It can also manifest as sleeping more or less or dreaming more.

Now that you understand a little more about the houses within your chart, you can perhaps make some sense out of what has manifested for you personally in 2020.

Transits

Here is an explanation for how each of the transits will impact us on a personal level. Refer to your personal chart to find the degree of each transit, and then you will have an accurate description of the area of your life that it has impacted upon based on the house it is in.

You may also find that these transits have aspected planets within your natal chart too, giving them much more intensity depending upon what planets they are. This is beyond the scope of this book to explore, and in order to know exactly how each transit affects you, a reading with a professional astrologer (such as myself) should be sought.

Saturn/Pluto conjunction at 22 degrees Capricorn - 6ᵗʰ – 14ᵗʰ January 2020

This conjunction was about the breakdown of something within your life. You will have felt it building throughout 2019 and then in January it reached its climax. There will be no doubts about the area of your life that Pluto has affected here. You will have seen it begin to break down early on in 2019 and it built up to the conjunction, as opposed to being a shock.

If it was in your seventh house this conjunction will force you to assess your long-term relationships on a deeper level and if you are not to lose them, you must put in the hard work required to keep them! If you are in a toxic relationship, then Pluto will help you to finally break free from it once and for all.

Another example might be if it manifested within your Ninth house. Superficial beliefs will be wiped away to be replaced with deeply rooted beliefs that are real and tangible. You might leave behind deeply held religious beliefs and have to rebuild your entire view of the spiritual side of life. All in all, this is one of the easier places for this conjunction to happen.

Although you may have lost something, or even some part of yourself during this time, it was a clearing of something that was no that was longer serving you, and even though Pluto's wrath is often painful, when you come out of the other side, you could begin to rebuild something new and more suited to who you are now.

Any transit with Saturn means that it is challenging and hard work. There is no getting away with it, to rebuild whatever is lost within your life will take time and dedication, there are no shortcuts. But the results will bring great rewards and Saturn always seeks to give you what you need in the end.

Jupiter and Pluto conjunction at 24 degrees – on April 5th and June 30th, and at 22 degrees on November 12th, 2020

The bottom line of this three-part conjunction is that will have marked you. A "mark" in my mind is an event that changes a person and therefore changes the rest of their life. For example, you are a child, and your parents get divorced (fourth house), or you are married, and your spouse dies (seventh or Eighth house). When these events happen, they mark you. They change you on every level.

They do not all have to be negative events. For example, you could get married (seventh house), or find out that you are pregnant (fifth house). The point to make is, that this transit will have had a huge impact in your life that will change the course of your journey in some way, and ultimately, change you as a person.

This is again due to the destructive nature of Pluto, but this time, in a meeting with Jupiter, everything is magnified and expanded. Jupiter is asking you, 'Where are you allowing yourself to settle?'. Jupiter wants you to believe in yourself and to make it happen! Pluto will helpfully push you along in that it will remove what is in your way! It can be a huge wake up call and force you down into the ashes where you will rise once more as a beautiful phoenix, never to look back.

Saturn conjunct Jupiter at 0 degrees of Aquarius – December 21st, 2020

A Great Conjunction represents a time for you to release old habits in order to make way for new ways of doing things. If you are not open to change, it can feel uncomfortable. But if you are, you can make incredible progress toward dreams you have held onto for a long time. The expansive nature of Jupiter and the structure of Saturn team up to help you accomplish something that may have felt out of reach before but is now totally within your grasp.

For instance, I have always wanted to write books, and when this conjunction happened in Aquarius, it fell within my fifth house of creativity and here I am, releasing my first book!

I would recommend choosing a special goal that has been calling to you for a while and spend as much time as you can in 2021 working toward it. If you really want something, you will feel extra motivated to do the work it takes to manifest it.

Since Jupiter and Saturn both have to do with professional achievements, this is great energy to channel toward career success. Whatever you decide to pursue will have Jupiter's accelerating force to kickstart growth in that area, plus the solid foundation of Saturn to ensure your results are long-lasting.

Uranus in Taurus square Saturn in Aquarius at 7 Degrees -

December 2020, 17th February, June, and December 2021

This transit will create a dynamic tension that will force you to transform your life in the area that you have these two planets.

This may have come as a shocking revelation for you as Uranus is about sudden and dramatic change that was not previously within your conscious awareness. However, things will not change overnight with this transit because of the nature of Taurus and Aquarius both being fixed signs, and Saturn is all about change through putting in the hard work.

Saturn-Uranus square will feel much like healing our wounds from the past, and once we have achieved this step, it will be our chance to grow into the next version of ourselves.

Conclusion

The purpose of this book was to provide you with a sense of clarity for the events of the past year. It was written for both novices and Astrology enthusiasts alike, and so my hope is that you have found it interesting but equally easy to follow.

We as a collective have to prepare ourselves for this new energy shift. It has been a long time coming and Saturn and Jupiter moving into Aquarius, and the element of Air, after an age of Earth transits will start to lead humanity in a new direction.

As individuals, we all have to hold ourselves accountable for the change we wish to see in the world to create a better world for our future. This is an exciting adventure, and I wish you all well on your own personal path of enlightenment.